LO QUE HACEN LOS BOMBEROS

WHAT FIREFIGHTERS DO

What Does a Community Helper Do? Bilingual

Erin Schmidt

Words to Know

bunker coat—Heavy coat worn to protect firefighters from heat.

bunker pants—Heavy pants worn to protect firefighters from heat.

community—A group of people who live in the same area.

dispatcher—A person who answers a 911 call and tells firefighters where to go.

pumper truck—Truck that pumps water through fire hoses.

siren—Loud alarm on a fire truck that tells other drivers to move out of the way.

sledgehammer—Large, heavy hammer used to punch through walls and knock open doors.

Palabras a conocer

el camión bomba—Camión que bombea agua a través de las mangueras contra incendio.

el chaquetón protector para bomberos—Chaqueta gruesa usada por los bomberos para protegerse del calor.

la comunidad—Un grupo de personas que viven en la misma área.

el despachador / la despachadora—Una persona que responde las llamadas que se hacen al 911 y le indica a los bomberos a dónde deben ir.

el mazo—Martillo grande y pesado usado para perforar paredes y abrir puertas.

los pantalones protectores para bomberos—Pantalones gruesos que usan los bomberos para protegerse del calor.

la sirena—Fuerte alarma del camión de bomberos que indica a los demás conductores que le dejen el camino libre.

Enslow Elementary

an imprint of

Enslow Publishers, Inc.

40 Industrial Road
Box 398
Berkeley Heights, NJ 07922
USA

http://www.enslow.com

Contents/Contenido

Words to Know
Palabras a conocer. 2

Fire!
¡Fuego! 5

Firefighters on the Way
Los bomberos en camino 7

What Do Firefighters Wear?
¿Qué ropa usan los bomberos? 9

What Do Firefighters Do?
¿Qué hacen los bomberos? 11

What Do Firefighters Use?
¿Qué utilizan los bomberos? 15

The Fire Is Out
El fuego se apagó 17

Firefighters Are Heroes
Los bomberos son héroes 21

Home Escape Plan
Plan de escape de una casa 22

Learn More / Más para aprender. 23

Index / Índice. 24

Some firefighters sleep at the fire station. They always have to be ready.

Algunos bomberos duermen en la estación de bomberos. Ellos tienen que estar siempre listos.

Fire!

Rrrring! Rrrring!

The alarm goes off at the fire station. The firefighters get out of bed. The dispatcher talks over the radio. She tells the firefighters that a house is burning.

• •

¡Fuego!

¡Rrrring! ¡Rrrring!

Suena la alarma en la estación de bomberos. Los bomberos se levantan de la cama. La despachadora habla por radio. Ella les dice a los bomberos que se ha incendiado una casa.

Firefighters have to know how to drive fire trucks.

Los bomberos tienen que saber cómo manejar los camiones de bomberos.

Firefighters on the Way

The firefighters rush to the fire trucks. The captain makes sure all the firefighters are ready to go. The driver turns on the flashing lights and sirens. He honks the horn to warn other drivers: "Move out of the way!"

· ·

Los bomberos en camino

Los bomberos corren a sus camiones. El capitán comprueba que todos los bomberos están listos para partir. El conductor enciende las luces intermitentes y las sirenas. Él toca el claxon para avisar a los demás conductores: "¡Quítense del camino!"

coat —
chaquetón

helmet
casco

pants
pantalones

boots
botas

Firefighters wear helmets, boots, coats, and pants to protect them from getting hurt.

Los bomberos usan cascos, botas, chaquetones y pantalones para protegerse del fuego.

What Do Firefighters Wear?

Firefighters put on special clothes to keep them safe. Helmets and hoods protect the firefighters' heads. Boots protect their feet. Bunker coats and bunker pants keep the firefighters from getting burned.

●●●●●●●●●●●●●●●●●●●●●●●●●●●●●●●●●●●●●●●

¿Qué ropa usan los bomberos?

Los bomberos usan ropa especial que los mantiene a salvo. Los cascos y las capuchas protegen la cabeza de los bomberos. Las botas protegen sus pies. Los chaquetones y pantalones protectores evitan que los bomberos se quemen.

Firefighters rescue people using long ladders.

Los bomberos rescatan a las personas usando escaleras largas.

What Do Firefighters Do?

The firefighters arrive at the scene. They check to make sure no people are in danger. They rescue people who are trapped. Firefighters help people who are hurt.

• •

¿Qué hacen los bomberos?

Los bombcros llegan a la escena. Ellos revisan para comprobar que no haya personas en peligro. Ellos rescatan a las personas que están atrapadas. Los bomberos ayudan a las personas que están heridas.

Every firefighter has a special job to do.

Cada bombero tiene una tarea especial que cumplir.

The fire chief gives each firefighter a job. One firefighter runs the pumper truck while another sprays water. Other firefighters climb ladders. Firefighters must work together to put out the fire.

• •

El jefe de los bomberos le da una tarea a cada bombero. Un bombero acciona el camión bomba, mientras otro echa el agua. Otros bomberos suben las escaleras. Los bomberos deben trabajar unidos para apagar el incendio.

axe
hacha

sledgehammer
mazo

fire hydrant wrench
llave del hidrante
contra incendio

fire hydrant
hidrante
contra
incendio

Firefighters use special tools.

Los bomberos usan herramientas
especiales.

What Do Firefighters Use?

Firefighters use special tools. An axe is used to chop holes. A sledgehammer is used to break open doors. A wrench is used to open fire hydrants.

• •

¿Qué utilizan los bomberos?

Los bomberos usan herramientas especiales. Se utiliza un hacha para abrir huecos. El mazo se usa para derribar puertas. Para abrir los hidrantes contra incendio ellos utilizan una llave.

Firefighters keep working even after the fire has been put out. They need to find out what caused the fire.

Los bomberos siguen trabajando aún después de apagar el incendio. Ellos necesitan descubrir qué causó el fuego.

The Fire Is Out

After the fire is out, the firefighters keep working. They spray more water to make sure the fire does not start again. They search to find why the fire started. Firefighters even help people find a new place to stay for the night.

• •

El fuego se apagó

Después que el fuego se apaga, los bomberos siguen trabajando. Ellos echan más agua para garantizar que el fuego no comience de nuevo. Ellos tratan de averiguar por qué empezó el fuego. Incluso, los bomberos ayudan a las personas a encontrar otro lugar donde pasar la noche.

Firefighters keep their trucks clean and shiny.

Los bomberos mantienen sus camiones limpios y brillantes.

Firefighters clean their tools, trucks, and clothes after a fire. They wash and load the hoses. They fill the fire truck tanks with water.

●●●●●●●●●●●●●●●●●●●●●●●●●●●●●●●●●●●●●●

Los bomberos limpian sus herramientas, camiones y ropas después de un incendio. Ellos lavan y guardan las mangueras. Ellos llenan de agua los tanques de los camiones de bomberos.

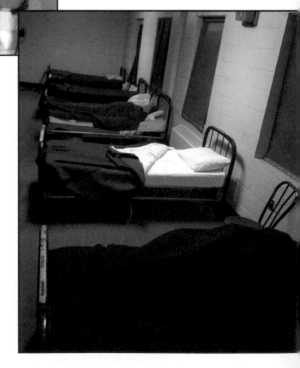

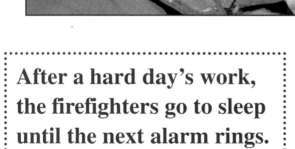

After a hard day's work, the firefighters go to sleep until the next alarm rings.

Después de un día difícil de trabajo, los bomberos van a dormir hasta que suene la próxima alarma.

Firefighters Are Heroes

When their work is done, the firefighters go back to the fire station. There they wait for the next fire alarm. Firefighters must always be ready to help. Firefighters are community heroes.

. . . .

Los bomberos son héroes

Cuando terminan su trabajo, los bomberos regresan a su cuartel. Allí esperan la siguiente alarma de incendio. Los bomberos siempre deben estar listos para ayudar. Los bomberos son héroes de la comunidad.

Home Escape Plan

Ask the adults you live with to help you make a home escape plan.

First, draw a map of your home. Draw lines to show two different ways to get out of your bedroom. In a real fire, you might need to leave your home through a window. Never go outside through your window unless it is an emergency.

Next, choose a safe place outside where you and your family can meet. Write the name of that place on your map. Post your escape plan on a bulletin board, wall, or refrigerator. Finally, hold a family fire drill to practice your escape plan.

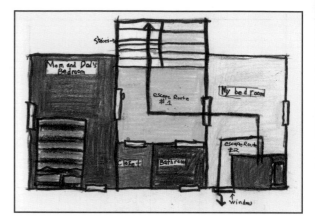

Plan de escape de una casa

Pide a los adultos con los cuales vives que te ayuden a hacer un plan de escape de tu casa.

Primero, dibuja un mapa de tu casa. Dibuja líneas que muestren dos formas diferentes de salir de tu cuarto. En un incendio de verdad puede ser que necesites salir de tu casa por una ventana. Nunca salgas por la ventana excepto en una emergencia.

A continuación, escoge un lugar seguro afuera, donde tú y tu familia puedan encontrarse. Escribe el nombre de ese lugar en tu mapa. Coloca tu plan de escape en una tablilla de noticias, la pared o el refrigerador. Finalmente, realiza un simulacro de incendio con tu familia para practicar tu plan de escape.

Learn More / Más para aprender

Books / Libros

In English/En inglés

Adamson, Heather. *A Day in the Life of a Firefighter*. Mankato, Minn.: Capstone Press, 2004.

Schaefer, Lola. *Who Works Here: Fire Station*. Chicago, Illinois: Heinemann Library, 2001.

In Spanish / En español

Catala, Ellen. *¿Qué hace un bombero?* Mankato, Minn.: Yellow Umbrella Books, 2005.

Miller, Heather. *Bombero*. Chicago, Ill.: Heinemann Library, 2003.

Internet Addresses / Direcciones de Internet

In English / En inglés

Sparky the Fire Dog
  <http://www.sparky.org>
  Learn about fire safety.

Welcome to the USFA's Kids Page: Where the Fun Starts
  <http://www.usfa.fema.gov/kids>
  Learn how you can be safe.

Index

alarm, 5, 20, 21
axe, 14, 15
boots, 8, 9
bunker coats, 8, 9
bunker pants, 8, 9
captain, 7

clothes, 9, 19
dispatcher, 5
fire chief, 13
fire hydrant, 14, 15
fire hydrant wrench, 14, 15

fire station, 4, 5, 21
fire trucks, 6, 7, 18, 19
helmets, 8, 9
hoods, 9
hoses, 19
ladders, 10, 13

pumper truck, 13
radio, 5
sirens, 7
sledgehammer, 14, 15
tools, 14, 15, 19
water, 13, 17, 19

Índice

agua, 13, 17, 19
alarma, 5, 20, 21
botas, 8, 9
camión bomba, 13
camiones de bomberos, 6, 7, 18, 19
capitán, 7

capuchas, 9
cascos, 8, 9
chaquetones protectores, 8, 9
despachadora, 5
escaleras, 10, 13
estación o cuartel de bomberos, 4, 5, 21

hacha, 14, 15
herramientas, 14, 15, 19
hidrante contra incendio, 14, 15
jefe de bomberos, 13
llave del hidrante contra incendio, 14, 15

mangueras, 19
mazo, 14, 15
pantalones protectores, 8, 9
radio, 5
ropa, 9, 19
sirenas, 7

• •

Note to Teachers and Parents: The *What Does a Community Helper Do?* series supports curriculum standards for K–4 learning about community services and helpers. The Words to Know section introduces subject-specific vocabulary. Early readers may require help with these new words.

Series Literacy Consultant:
Allan A. De Fina, Ph.D.
Past President of the New Jersey Reading Association
Professor, Department of Literacy Education
New Jersey City University

• •

Enslow Elementary, an imprint of Enslow Publishers, Inc.

Enslow Elementary® is a registered trademark of Enslow Publishers, Inc.

Bilingual edition copyright 2008 by Enslow Publishers, Inc. Originally published in English under the title *What Does a Firefighter Do?* © 2005 by Enslow Publishers, Inc. Bilingual edition translated by Eloísa X. Le Riverend, edited by Susana C. Schultz, of Strictly Spanish, LLC.

Copyright © 2008 by Enslow Publishers, Inc.

Library of Congress Cataloging-in-Publication Data

Schmidt, Erin.
    [What does a firefighter do? Spanish & English]
    Lo que hacen los bomberos = What firefighters do / Erin Schmidt.
        p. cm. — (What does a community helper do?)
    Includes bibliographical references and index.
    ISBN-13: 978-0-7660-2826-5
    ISBN-10: 0-7660-2826-7
    1. Fire extinction—Juvenile literature. 2. Fire fighters—Juvenile literature. I. Title. II. Title: What firefighters do.
    TH9148.S3518 2007
    628.9'25—dc22   2006019232

Printed in the United States of America
10 9 8 7 6 5 4 3 2 1

To Our Readers:
We have done our best to make sure all Internet Addresses in this book were active and appropriate when we went to press. However, the author and the publisher have no control over and assume no liability for the material available on those Internet sites or on other Web sites they may link to. Any comments or suggestions can be sent by e-mail to comments@enslow.com or to the address on the back cover.

Every effort has been made to locate all copyright holders of material used in this book. If any errors or omissions have occurred, corrections will be made in future editions of this book.

Illustration Credits: Comstock Images/Getty Images, p. 8 (center); © Royalty-Free/CORBIS, p. 16; Creatas, p. 1; Adam Crowley/PhotoDisc/Getty Images, p. 6; Enslow Publishers, Inc., p. 22; Hemera Technologies, Inc. 1997–2000, pp. 2, 8 (objects around center photograph), 13, 14 (all), 19; Mark C. Ide, pp. 4, 18, 20 (bottom); Skip Nall/PhotoDisc/Getty Images, p. 12; Leslie O'Shaughnessy/ Visuals Unlimited, p. 10; Thinkstock/Getty Images, p. 20 (top).

Cover credits: Creatas (bottom); top left to right (Skip Nall/PhotoDisc/Getty Images, p. 12; Corel Corporation; Mark C. Ide; Leslie O'Shaughnessy/Visuals Unlimited.)